THE "SWEET TREATS FOR LITTLE CHEFS" COOKBOOK IS THE PERFECT GUIDE FOR KIDS WHO LOVE TO BAKE AND HAVE A SWEET TOOTH. THIS COOKBOOK IS FILLED WITH FUN AND EASY-TO-FOLLOW DESSERT RECIPES THAT ARE PERFECT FOR KIDS TO MAKE ON THEIR OWN OR WITH THE HELP OF AN ADULT.

FROM CLASSIC CHOCOLATE CHIP COOKIES AND BROWNIES TO CREATIVE AND UNIQUE DESSERTS LIKE ICE CREAM SANDWICHES AND CAKE POPS, THIS COOKBOOK HAS SOMETHING FOR EVERYONE. THE RECIPES ARE DESIGNED TO BE KID-FRIENDLY WITH SIMPLE INGREDIENTS AND EASY-TO-FOLLOW INSTRUCTIONS. PLUS, EACH RECIPE INCLUDES COLORFUL PICTURES THAT WILL INSPIRE KIDS TO GET CREATIVE IN THE KITCHEN.

THE "SWEET TREATS FOR LITTLE CHEFS" COOKBOOK NOT ONLY PROVIDES DELICIOUS RECIPES, BUT IT ALSO TEACHES KIDS VALUABLE SKILLS IN THE KITCHEN SUCH AS MEASURING INGREDIENTS, MIXING BATTER, AND DECORATING DESSERTS. IT'S A GREAT WAY TO SPEND QUALITY TIME WITH FAMILY AND FRIENDS WHILE CREATING TASTY TREATS THAT EVERYONE WILL LOVE.

OVERALL, THIS COOKBOOK IS A MUST-HAVE FOR ANY KID WHO LOVES TO BAKE AND WANTS TO EXPLORE THEIR CREATIVE SIDE IN THE KITCHEN.

Avocado Brownies

Avocado brownies are a delicious, healthy alternative to traditional brownies. They're loaded with nutrients and have the same fudgy, rich texture as classic brownies. Plus, they're easy to make! Here's how:

First, preheat your oven to 350 degrees Fahrenheit. Then grab all of your ingredients - 1 medium ripe avocado, 1/2 cup maple syrup, 2 large eggs, 1 tsp vanilla extract, ½ cup oat flour (about 60g), ¼ cup cocoa powder, ½ tsp baking soda and ¼ cup chocolate chips (optional).

Next, mash the avocado in a bowl until it's creamy. Add the maple syrup, eggs and vanilla extract to the avocado and mix until everything is thoroughly combined.

In a separate bowl, combine the oat flour, cocoa powder and baking soda. Slowly add this to the wet ingredients in the other bowl, stirring as you go. Once everything is mixed together evenly, fold in the chocolate chips (if desired).

Pour the mixture into a greased 8x8 inch baking pan. Bake for 20-25 minutes until a toothpick inserted into the center comes out clean. Let cool before cutting into bars and serving. Enjoy!

These avocado brownies make a great healthy dessert option for kids, especially when served with some fresh fruit. They also make a great snack or after-school treat. So next time you're looking for a delicious, healthy dessert recipe, try these easy avocado brownies! You won't be disappointed.

Banana Sushi

If you're looking for a healthy and fun dessert recipe for kids, try this delicious banana sushi! It's easy to prepare and makes a great snack or after-dinner treat.

To get started, simply place a ripe banana on a platter and slice it into "sushi" pieces. Then, drizzle the pieces with melted peanut butter and sprinkle them with chopped strawberries, mini chocolate chips, and crushed graham crackers. Give the platter a final garnish with some edible flowers or fresh mint leaves, if desired.

This easy treat is sure to be a hit with kids of all ages! Not only is it fun to prepare, but it's also a healthy alternative to more sugary desserts. Plus, the ingredients are simple and easy to find in any grocery store.

So go ahead and give this delicious banana sushi a try- it's sure to be a hit in your home! Enjoy!

Honey And Lime Grilled Pineapple

Ingredients

1 pineapple.
2 Tbsp honey or maple syrup for vegan option.
1 Tbsp lime juice.
4 Tbsp unsweetened shredded coconut.
Recommended for serving: coconut ice cream or sorbet.

This delicious and healthy dessert is perfect for kids and adults alike! Grilled pineapple with honey, lime, and coconut is an easy way to make a sweet treat that's full of flavor.

To prepare this dish, start by cutting a pineapple into slices about 1/2 inch thick. Place the slices on a heated grill or griddle and cook for about two minutes on each side, or until the pineapple starts to caramelize. Once the pineapple is golden brown, remove from the heat and place in a bowl. Drizzle honey (or maple syrup if vegan) and lime juice over the pineapple slices, then sprinkle with shredded coconut.

For serving, you can either enjoy the grilled pineapple on its own or with a scoop of coconut ice cream or sorbet. Not only is this healthy dessert delicious and refreshing, it's also packed with essential vitamins and minerals that are important for good health. Whether you're looking for a special treat to reward your kids or just want something sweet without all the added sugar, honey and lime grilled pineapple is sure to be a hit! Enjoy!
!

Blueberry Muffins

Ingredients

1 ½ cups all-purpose flour. Great Value All-Purpose Flour, 5LB Bag.
¾ cup white sugar.
2 teaspoons baking powder.
½ teaspoon salt.
⅓ cup vegetable oil.
1 egg.
⅓ cup milk, or more as needed.
1 cup fresh blueberries.

Making a batch of delicious and healthy blueberry muffins is easy with the right ingredients. To begin, preheat your oven to 375°F (190°C). In a large bowl, combine 1 ½ cups all-purpose flour, ¾ cup white sugar, 2 teaspoons baking powder and ½ teaspoon salt. Add ⅓ cup vegetable oil and mix with a wooden spoon until the dry ingredients are moistened. Beat in 1 egg, then stir in ⅓ cup of milk. Gently fold in 1 cup fresh blueberries for a hint of sweetness and color.

Line your muffin tin with paper liners or spray it with cooking spray and fill each cup three-quarters full with the batter. Bake in preheated oven for 18 to 20 minutes, or until a toothpick inserted into the center of a muffin comes out clean. Let cool and enjoy your homemade blueberry muffins!

These healthy blueberry muffins are perfect as a snack or dessert, especially when baking with kids. They also make a great addition to a lunchbox and are sure to be a hit with the little ones! With this simple recipe, you can create tasty and nutritious treats in no time. So next time your family is looking for something sweet, whip up a batch of these blueberry muffins for an easy and healthy dessert. Enjoy!

Baked Donuts

Are you looking for a delicious and healthy dessert that kids are sure to love? Baked donuts might be the perfect treat! To make them, you'll need some simple ingredients: 4 tablespoons (57g) of butter, 1/4 cup (50g) of vegetable oil, 1/2 cup (99g) of granulated sugar, 1/3 cup (71g) of light brown sugar or dark brown sugar packed, 2 large eggs, 1 1/2 teaspoons baking powder, 1/4 teaspoon baking soda and ½ to 1 teaspoon nutmeg.

To prepare the donuts, preheat your oven to 350°F (175°C). In a medium-sized bowl, cream together the butter and sugars until light and fluffy. Add in the eggs one at a time, beating well after each addition. In a separate bowl, mix together all of the dry ingredients - baking powder, baking soda and nutmeg. Gradually add the dry ingredients to the wet ingredients, mixing until combined.

Using a spoon, drop the dough into lightly greased donut pans. Bake for 8 to 10 minutes, or until golden brown. Let the donuts cool completely before serving. Enjoy! Baked donuts are a fun and tasty treat that kids will love, and they're great for healthy dessert recipes too!

Cereal Yoghurt Bars

This delicious cereal yoghurt bar is the perfect treat for kids and adults alike. To make this easy and healthy dessert, start by preheating your oven to 350°F. In a large bowl, combine 2 cups of grape nuts cereal, ¾ cup of all-purpose flour, ¼ cup of brown sugar, and ½ teaspoon of cinnamon. Cut in ½ cup of margarine, and mix until crumbly. Press the mixture into an 8x8 inch greased baking pan, and bake for 15 minutes or until golden brown.

In a separate bowl, combine 1 container of BREYERS Strawberry low-fat yogurt with 1 large egg (slightly beaten). Add 2 tablespoons of all-purpose flour, and mix until fully combined. Spread the yogurt mixture over the cereal crust in the baking pan, and bake for an additional 20 minutes, or until lightly browned. Let cool before cutting into bars. Enjoy your homemade cereal yoghurt bars as a tasty and healthy dessert!

This recipe is great for kids' parties and other special occasions, as it's both flavorful and healthy. Plus, you can customize the ingredients to make your own unique version of this dessert! So, get creative in the kitchen with these cereal yoghurt bars, and enjoy a delicious treat that everyone can love.

Chocolate Peanut Butter Avocado Pudding

This healthy chocolate peanut butter avocado pudding is the perfect way to indulge your sweet tooth while providing a healthy treat for you and your family. It's easy to make and requires minimal ingredients: 1 1/2 ripe avocados, 1 large ripe banana, 1/2 cup unsweetened cocoa or cacao powder, 1/2 cup salted creamy or crunchy peanut butter (plus more for topping), and ~1/2 cup sweetener of choice such as maple syrup, agave, date paste or honey if not vegan.

To prepare the pudding, start by peeling and mashing the avocados until smooth. Then add in the banana, cocoa powder, peanut butter, and sweetener of choice and blend until completely combined. Pour the pudding into individual bowls or jars for serving, garnish with additional peanut butter, and enjoy! This delicious pudding is perfect for a healthy dessert option for kids and adults alike.

Enjoy your homemade chocolate peanut butter avocado pudding! It's sure to be a hit with the whole family.

Happy eating!

Cookie Dough

Ingredients
- 2-1/2 cups butter, softened.
- 2 cups sugar.
- 2 large eggs, room temperature.
- 1/4 cup 2% milk.
- 2 teaspoons vanilla extract.
- 7-1/2 to 8 cups (30 to 32 oz.) all-purpose flour.
- 4 teaspoons baking powder.
- 1 teaspoon salt.

Using the above ingredients, you can make a delicious batch of cookie dough for your family. To properly prepare the cookie dough, begin by creaming together the butter and sugar in a large bowl until light and fluffy. Next, add in the eggs one at a time, followed by milk and vanilla extract. Mix until combined. In a separate bowl
, sift together the flour, baking powder and salt before gradually stirring into the wet ingredients until completely incorporated. Now your cookie dough is ready to be used for your favorite healthy dessert recipes! Whether you're making cookies for a school bake sale or just looking for some fun activities for kids, this simple recipe will help make it a breeze. With only a few ingredients and minimal preparation time, you can easily make a batch of delicious homemade cookie dough that everyone will love. Enjoy!

Almond Brownie

Ingredients

Butter - I use salted, but you can also use unsalted butter and add an extra ¼ teaspoon salt to the batter.
Eggs - Large eggs are what I use.
Sugar.
All-Purpose Flour.
Salt.
Baking Powder.
Almond Extract - 1 tablespoon sounds like a lot, but it's just right!
Sliced Almonds.

This almond brownie recipe is simple to prepare and makes a delicious, healthy dessert for kids. To make it, you'll need butter, eggs, sugar, all-purpose flour, salt, baking powder, almond extract and sliced almonds. Start by preheating the oven to 350°F. Grease an 8x8 inch pan and set aside. In a medium bowl, cream together the butter and sugar until light and fluffy. Add in the eggs one at a time, beating until fully combined. Add in the almond extract, flour, baking powder, and salt. Stir until no streaks of flour remain. Gradually fold in the almonds. Spread the batter evenly into the greased pan. Bake for 25 minutes or until a toothpick inserted into the center comes out clean. Let cool before cutting and serving. Enjoy!

Apple Crisp

Ingredients

10 cups all-purpose apples, peeled, cored and sliced.
1 cup white sugar. Great Value Pure Granulated Sugar, 4 lb.
1 tablespoon all-purpose flour.
1 teaspoon ground cinnamon.
½ cup water.
1 cup quick-cooking oats.
1 cup all-purpose flour.
1 cup packed brown sugar.

Apple crisp is a delicious, healthy dish that makes for a great dessert recipe for kids. To prepare an apple crisp, you will need 10 cups of peeled and cored apples sliced into thin pieces. You can then combine the apples with 1 cup of white sugar, 1 tablespoon of all-purpose flour, 1 teaspoon of ground cinnamon, and ½ cup of water in a large bowl. In a separate bowl, combine 1 cup of quick-cooking oats, 1 cup of all-purpose flour and 1 cup of packed brown sugar. Sprinkle this mixture over the apples and mix it together gently until everything is evenly coated. Place the mixture into an 8x8 inch baking pan or dish and bake at 375 degrees Fahrenheit for 30-40 minutes until the top is golden brown. Enjoy your delicious apple crisp!

Apple crisp is a healthy dish that kids will love and it's easy to make. Not only does this recipe provide a great way for kids to get their daily intake of fruit, but it also provides them with the necessary vitamins and minerals they need to stay healthy. With just a few simple ingredients, you can make a delicious apple crisp that everyone will enjoy. So why not try out this tasty dessert recipe today? You won't regret it! Enjoy!

Almond Butter Blossom

Ingredients

1/2 cup creamy almond butter.
1/2 cup butter, softened.
1/2 cup granulated sugar.
1/2 cup packed brown sugar.
1 egg.
1 1/2 cups Gold Medal™ all-purpose flour.
3/4 teaspoon baking soda.
1/2 teaspoon baking powder.

Almond Butter Blossoms are a delicious and healthy dessert that kids will love. With only a few simple ingredients, you can whip up these sweet treats in no time!

To start, preheat your oven to 375 degrees F (190 C). Next, cream together the almond butter and softened butter until light and fluffy. Add in both the granulated sugar and brown sugar and beat until combined. Add in the egg and mix well.

In a separate bowl, combine the flour, baking soda, and baking powder. Gradually add this to the butter mixture and stir until all ingredients are incorporated.

Roll tablespoon-sized scoops of cookie dough into balls and place onto an ungreased baking sheet. Bake for 8-10 minutes, or until lightly golden brown. Allow the cookies to cool on the baking sheet before transferring them to a wire rack to cool completely.

These Almond Butter Blossoms are perfect for kids who are looking for healthy dessert recipes that still offer plenty of sweetness! The combination of nutty almond butter and soft, chewy cookies is sure to please both young and old alike. Enjoy!

Avocado Chocolate Truffles

Ingredients
⅔ cup mashed avocado, about 1 avocado.
1 cup dark chocolate chips, I like Lily's chocolate chips.
pinch sea salt.
2-3 Tablespoons cocoa powder.

Avocado and chocolate is an unexpected combination, but with these delicious avocado chocolate truffles, you can make a healthy dessert that even kids will love. To prepare the truffles, first mash the avocado until it's smooth and creamy. Then melt the dark chocolate chips in a double boiler or microwave-safe bowl. Once melted, stir in the mashed avocado and a pinch of sea salt. Next, stir in the cocoa powder until well combined. Allow the mixture to cool for about 10 minutes before forming into balls with your hands. Place the truffles on a parchment-lined baking sheet and refrigerate them for at least an hour or two before serving—or overnight if you want them to be extra firm. Enjoy these delicious and healthy avocado chocolate truffles as a sweet treat that kids will love!

Yogurt Muffins

Ingredients

2 cups (275g) good quality flour.
2 tsp. baking powder.
1/2 tsp baking soda.
pinch of salt.
1/2 cup (100g) sugar.
2 eggs.
1/2 cup (100ml) light olive oil.
1 cup (250ml) unsweetened yogurt (if using Greek yogurt, add 1 tbsp milk or buttermilk)

We all know how difficult it is to find healthy dessert recipes for kids. But, that doesn't mean you can't make delicious treats that are both tasty and nutritious! These Yogurt Muffins are sure to be a hit with the entire family.

To prepare these muffins, start by preheating your oven to 350°F (180°C). In a large bowl, combine the flour, baking powder, baking soda, and salt. In a separate bowl, mix together the sugar, eggs and oil. Add this mixture to the dry ingredients in the other bowl and stir until just combined.

Now add the yogurt and fold into the batter until it's just combined. Lightly grease a muffin tin and fill each cup with the batter. Bake for 18-20 minutes, or until a toothpick inserted into the center comes out clean. Let cool before serving.

These Yogurt Muffins are a great healthy dessert option that your kids will love! Enjoy!

Banana Pancakes

Ingredients
350g self-raising flour.
1 tsp baking powder.
2 very ripe bananas.
2 medium eggs.
1 tsp vanilla extract.
250ml whole milk.
butter, for frying.

Banana Pancakes are a delicious and healthy treat that kids of all ages will love! With only 7 simple ingredients, these pancakes are easy to make, packed full of nutrients and flavour.

To start with, in a large bowl mix together the self-raising flour and baking powder. Next, mash up the two very ripe bananas until it is creamy. Add this to the dry ingredients along with the eggs and vanilla extract. Slowly pour in the milk whilst stirring continuously. Once all your ingredients have been combined you should be left with a thick batter consistency.

Heat up some butter in a non-stick frying pan on medium heat before spooning tablespoons of pancake batter onto the pan. Let each pancake cook for approximately two minutes, flipping when the batter starts to bubble. Serve with your favourite topping and enjoy!

Banana Pancakes are full of energy-boosting ingredients that kids need to grow strong and healthy. Bananas are a great source of vitamins B6 and C, as well as dietary fibre which is important for digestive health. The eggs provide high quality protein which helps muscles repair and replenish energy stores. And lastly, whole milk contains beneficial fats, carbohydrates and micronutrients that support overall health.

So why not give Banana Pancakes a try this weekend? They're both healthy and delicious - a winning combination! Enjoy!

No Sugar Banana Bread

Ingredients

4 very ripe bananas.
2 eggs.
1/2 cup olive oil.
1/4 cup milk.
1 tsp vanilla bean paste.
1 tsp Coles Cinnamon Ground.
1 cup wholemeal flour.
1 cup plain flour.

This delicious no sugar banana bread recipe is perfect for kids who want a healthy dessert. It's easy to make and uses simple ingredients you likely already have in your pantry or refrigerator.

To make this no sugar banana bread, start by preheating the oven to 180°C (350°F). Then, mash together the bananas until they are smooth and creamy. In a separate bowl, beat together eggs, olive oil, milk, vanilla bean paste and Coles Cinnamon Ground until combined.

Add both wholemeal flour and plain flour to the wet ingredients, stirring well until fully incorporated. Finally, fold in the mashed bananas until combined before pouring into a greased and lined loaf tin. Bake for 45 minutes or until a skewer inserted into the centre comes out clean.

This no sugar banana bread is full of flavour and makes for a healthy treat that kids will love! Enjoy with your family or serve with yoghurt or ice-cream for an extra special dessert. Delicious!

Blueberry Ricotta Pound Cake

Ingredients

1 ⅔ Cups (205 g) All-Purpose Flour.
1 Tablespoon Baking Powder.
1 teaspoon Sea Salt.
1 ⅔ Cups (370 g) Whole Milk Ricotta.
¾ Cup (170 g) Unsalted Butter, softened.
1 ½ Cups (300 g) Granulated Sugar.
1 Lemon's worth of zest.
3 (150 g) Eggs, large.

This Blueberry Ricotta Pound Cake is a delicious and healthy dessert for kids. It's packed with creamy ricotta cheese and bursting with fresh blueberries. The cake is made using all-purpose flour, baking powder, sea salt, whole milk ricotta, unsalted butter, granulated sugar, lemon zest, and eggs. The combination of these ingredients creates a moist and fluffy pound cake that your kids will love! For added flavor and texture, top the cake off with some extra fresh or frozen blueberries. Serve it as an after-dinner treat or enjoy it for breakfast! No matter when you have it, this Blueberry Ricotta Pound Cake is sure to be enjoyed by all. Enjoy!

Happy baking!

Fried Apple Pie Rolls

Fried apple pie rolls are a delicious treat that the whole family will enjoy! They're made with just seven simple ingredients and are perfect for dessert or an after-school snack. Start by melting two tablespoons of butter in a skillet over medium heat. Add five cups of diced, peeled Granny Smith apples to the skillet. Sprinkle four tablespoons of sugar and one ¼ teaspoons of ground cinnamon on top, followed by a pinch each of nutmeg and salt. Mix everything together, stirring occasionally until the apples begin to soften (about 8 minutes). Once softened, add one tablespoon of all-purpose flour and two teaspoons lemon juice to the mixture. Stir everything together and cook for another 2 minutes until the mixture is thickened. To assemble the rolls, spoon two tablespoons of the apple mixture onto a sheet of store-bought puff pastry. Roll up the pastry tightly and brush the tops with melted butter. Place onto a baking sheet lined with parchment paper and bake for about 20 minutes or until golden brown. Serve warm with a scoop of vanilla ice cream for an extra special treat!

Fried apple pie rolls are an easy way to satisfy your sweet tooth without all the added sugar. Kids will love helping out in the kitchen as they assemble these delicious treats! Enjoy them warm from the oven or cooled off - either way, they're sure to be a hit at your next family gathering. So what are you waiting for? Get those apples rolling!

Cinnamon Oatmeal Cookies!

Ingredients

1 cup butter, softened. Great Value Sweet Cream Salted Butter, 16 oz.
1 cup brown sugar.
2 eggs.
1 teaspoon vanilla extract.
1 ½ cups all-purpose flour.
1 teaspoon baking soda.
1 teaspoon salt.
1 teaspoon ground cinnamon.

These Cinnamon Oatmeal Cookies are an easy, healthy snack or dessert for the whole family. They have a delicious combination of buttery sweetness, oat-y goodness and just the right amount of cinnamon spice. With only 6 basic ingredients, they are sure to become a favorite in your household!

To make these yummy treats, start by creaming together 1 cup of softened butter with 1 cup of brown sugar until light and fluffy. Add 2 eggs and 1 teaspoon of vanilla extract and beat until well combined. In a separate bowl, combine 1 ½ cups all-purpose flour, 1 teaspoon baking soda, 1 teaspoon salt and 1 teaspoon ground cinnamon. Gradually add the dry ingredients to the wet mixture and mix until just incorporated.

Drop tablespoon-sized dollops of dough onto an ungreased baking sheet and bake at 350°F for 10 - 12 minutes or until golden brown. Allow to cool before serving and enjoy! These cookies are the perfect snack or dessert for all your family gatherings. Enjoy!

Crispy Peanut Butter Balls

Ingredients
½ cup butter, softened.
2 cups creamy peanut butter.
3 cups powdered sugar.
3 cups crispy rice cereal, more for garnish.
2 cups chocolate chunk, preferably dark, for coating.

These delicious peanut butter balls are the perfect healthy treat for kids! With simple ingredients like creamy peanut butter, crispy rice cereal and dark chocolate chunks, you'll be giving them a powerful combination of vitamins, minerals and antioxidants.

Start by combining the softened butter with your favorite creamy peanut butter. Mix together until it forms a smooth paste. Then stir in powdered sugar until everything is well incorporated.

Next add 3 cups of crispy rice cereal and mix it all together. You can always add more if you want your peanut butter balls to have an extra crunchy texture. After that, use your hands to roll the mixture into small balls about 1 inch in size and place them on a parchment lined baking sheet. Allow the peanut butter balls to cool in the refrigerator for 30 minutes.

Once chilled, it's time to coat them with chocolate! Place 2 cups of dark chocolate chunks into a microwave safe bowl and heat on high for 1 minute, stirring every 20 seconds until melted. Dip each peanut butter ball into the melted chocolate, then gently shake off any excess and place onto a parchment lined baking sheet. Sprinkle some extra crispy rice cereal over top and set the sheet back in the fridge for another 10 minutes or until hardened.

And that's how you make yummy and healthy crispy peanut butter balls! Enjoy!

Pineapple Ice Cream

Pineapple Ice Cream is a delicious and healthy way to indulge in a cold treat on hot summer days. Not only is it packed with juicy fresh pineapple, but also has sweetened condensed milk and heavy whipping cream for an extra creamy texture.

To make this tasty dessert, you'll need 5 cups of chopped fresh pineapple (2 lb., 1 oz.), 1 1/2 cups cold heavy whipping cream, and 1 (14-oz.) can of sweetened condensed milk. Begin by adding all ingredients into a blender and blending until the mixture reaches an even consistency. Then pour the mixture into your ice cream maker and follow the instructions to freeze it.

Once the Pineapple Ice Cream is finished, scoop it out into individual bowls or cones. You can top it off with some extra pineapple wedges for a fruity finish. Enjoy!

This Pineapple Ice Cream is the perfect summer snack to share with kids and adults alike. It's a sweet treat that won't break your diet goals - just be sure to enjoy it in moderation. Bon appetit!

Chocolate Zucchini Brownie

These Chocolate Zucchini Brownies are a delicious, healthy dessert for kids! They're packed with zucchini, sweetened with sugar and flavored with vanilla extract. Plus, they've got a rich cocoa flavor from the unsweetened cocoa powder. To make these brownies you'll need 1 ½ cups of white sugar, ½ cup vegetable oil, 2 teaspoons vanilla extract, 2 cups all-purpose flour, ½ cup unsweetened cocoa powder, 1 ½ teaspoons baking soda and 1 teaspoon salt. Then simply stir in 2 cups of shredded zucchini to give your brownies an extra boost of nutrition without losing any flavor. Bake them up in the oven at 350°F for 25-30 minutes until golden brown and bubbling. When they're done, let them cool for a few minutes before cutting into squares and serving. Enjoy!

These Chocolate Zucchini Brownies are the perfect way to satisfy your sweet tooth while sneakily getting in some vegetables. Enjoy this delicious dessert with the whole family!

Almond Honey Power Bar

Ingredients
1 cup old-fashioned rolled oats.
¼ cup slivered almonds.
¼ cup sunflower seeds.
1 tablespoon flaxseeds, preferably golden.
1 tablespoon sesame seeds.
1 cup unsweetened whole-grain puffed cereal (see Note)
⅓ cup currants.
⅓ cup chopped dried apricots.

These Almond Honey Power Bars are a delicious and nutritious snack that your kids will love! A perfect lunchbox treat or after school snack, these bars are packed with healthy ingredients like oats, almonds, sunflower seeds, flaxseeds, sesame seeds, unsweetened whole-grain puffed cereal, currants and dried apricots. They're sweetened naturally with honey for a hint of sweetness without any added sugar. Not only do they taste great – they provide an energy boost too! So why not get the kids involved in making them? It's sure to be a fun activity that your little ones will enjoy. With just 10 minutes or prepping time and 20 minutes to bake in the oven, these Almond Honey Power Bars can be on the table in no time! Enjoy a tasty and healthy snack that both kids and adults will love.

For more healthy dessert recipes, check out our blog for creative ideas that your family will love! From wholesome muffins to scrumptious cakes, there's something for everyone. Let us help you find new ways to make dessert-time healthier and more enjoyable today! Happy baking!

No Bake Peanut Butter Cookies

Ingredients
3 cups white sugar. Great Value Pure Granulated Sugar, 4 lb.
¾ cup butter.
¾ cup milk.
1 ½ cups peanut butter.
½ teaspoon vanilla extract.
4 ½ cups quick-cooking oats.

No bake peanut butter cookies are a healthy dessert the whole family will love, and they're perfect for those busy weeknights when you don't have time to bake! All you need is few simple ingredients such as Great Value Pure Granulated Sugar, butter, milk, peanut butter, vanilla extract, and quick-cooking oats. In just a few short minutes, you can whip up this delicious treat that kids of all ages will appreciate.

To make no bake peanut butter cookies: In a large saucepan over medium heat, bring 3 cups white sugar and ¾ cup butter to a light boil for 2 minutes. Once the mixture has boiled for 2 minutes remove from heat and add in the ¾ cup milk, 1 ½ cups peanut butter, and ½ teaspoon vanilla extract. Stir until the mixture is smooth.

Next, gradually add in 4 ½ cups quick-cooking oats and stir until everything is evenly combined. Drop spoonfuls of the cookie dough onto wax paper to cool completely before serving. Enjoy!

These no bake peanut butter cookies are a simple and delicious dessert that can be made in no time at all! It's time to treat your family to a healthy sweet treat everyone will love. Make some no bake peanut butter cookies today!

Granola Bars

Granola bars are a great way to give your kids a healthy snack that's also delicious. This recipe is an easy one that kids will love, and it features natural peanut butter or cashew butter, honey and whole rolled oats as the main ingredients. You can add in mini chocolate chips for extra sweetness (if desired) and top with some pepitas, crushed peanuts or cashews for crunch. With this simple recipe you can have homemade granola bars ready in no time! Enjoy!

To make the granola bars, start by combining 1 cup of natural peanut butter or cashew butter, 2/3 cup honey and 1 teaspoon vanilla extract in a saucepan over medium heat. Stir until everything is combined and then remove the pan from the heat. In a separate bowl, combine 2 ½ cups of whole rolled oats with heaping ½ teaspoon sea salt. Mix well. Pour the peanut butter mixture into the bowl with the oats and mix together until everything is well incorporated. If desired, add in 1/3 cup mini chocolate chips for extra sweetness. Scoop out a spoonful at a time onto parchment paper or wax paper on a baking sheet. Flatten each spoonful to form bar shapes. Sprinkle with pepitas, crushed peanuts or cashews. Allow the bars to cool and set before serving. Enjoy!

Granola bars are a great way to give your kids a healthy snack that's not only delicious but also easy to make at home. With this simple recipe you can have homemade granola bars ready in no time! Enjoy!

Cinnamon Apple Pie

Cinnamon apple pie is a delicious and healthy dessert recipe that kids will love! It's made with simple ingredients that you can find in any grocery store. To start, gather the pastry dough for a 2-crust pie, 1 cup light brown sugar, 1/2 teaspoon of cinnamon, 4 tablespoons of flour, 6 cups peeled and cored thinly sliced apples, 1 tablespoon of lemon juice and 2 tablespoons of butter cut into small cubes. If desired you can also use an egg beaten with one tablespoon of water to brush over the crust before baking.

Begin by preheating your oven to 375 degrees F (190 degrees C). Grease a 9 inch pie dish and roll out half the pastry dough for the bottom crust. Place in the dish and trim the edges. In a large bowl combine the sugar, cinnamon, flour and apples. Stir to coat the apples evenly with mixture. Pour into the pastry lined pie dish and sprinkle with lemon juice. Dot with butter cubes. Roll out remaining crust and place over top of filling; trim edges, seal, and flute or crimp as desired. If using egg wash, brush top crust lightly before baking.

Bake for 40 to 45 minutes or until golden brown on top. Cover outer edge of crust with foil if it's getting too dark while baking (it will be done before then but you don't want it to burn!). Allow pie to cool completely before slicing and serving! Enjoy this delicious cinnamon apple pie with a scoop of ice cream or a dollop of whipped cream.

Happy baking! :)

For an even healthier twist, you can choose to use whole wheat pastry flour instead of all-purpose white flour and replace the light brown sugar with coconut sugar. This will add more fiber to your recipe and reduce its glycemic index. Coconut sugar is also less processed than regular white or brown sugars, making it better for your body overall! For a vegan version, simply use a non-dairy butter replacement like Earth Balance in place of traditional butter. No matter what tweaks you make, this cinnamon apple pie will still be delicious every time! Enjoy! :)

Strawberry Cheesecake

Creating a delicious strawberry cheesecake couldn't be easier! Start by creaming together cream cheese and sugar. Then, add in sour cream and mix until everything is well blended. Finally, pour the mixture into a pre-baked crust and bake for 25 minutes.

To make the heavenly strawberry sauce to top your cheesecake, start by mashing fresh strawberries with a fork or potato masher. Add some sugar to taste and cook over medium heat until it thickens. Spread this delightful strawberry topping over your finished baked cheesecake and enjoy!

This healthy dessert recipe is sure to please kids of all ages - they'll love the sweet strawberry flavor paired with creamy cheesecake texture! Plus, it's an excellent way to introduce them to the joys of baking desserts. Enjoy!

Baked Churros

Churros are a great way to make healthy dessert recipes for kids! The batter is easy to whip up and contains just six simple ingredients you're likely to have in your pantry or fridge. All you need is butter, flour, salt, water, eggs, sugar and some vanilla extract for added flavor. Once the batter is cooked it can be cut into strips and deep fried until it's crisp on the outside and fluffy on the inside. Serve with a sprinkle of cinnamon sugar and some fresh fruit or plain yogurt for a nutritious treat everyone will love! Enjoy!

Fruitcake

Ingredients

1 1/2 cups (213g) dried pineapple, diced.
1 1/2 cups (255g) raisins, golden or regular.
1 cup (128g) dried apricots, diced.
1 1/2 cups (223g) dates, chopped.
heaping 1 cup (170g) candied red cherries, plus additional for decoration, if desired.
1/3 cup (64g) crystallized ginger, diced, optional.

Fruitcake is a classic dessert that kids are sure to love! It's made from dried fruits, such as pineapple, raisins, apricots, dates and cherries. To give it an extra zing of flavor and fun for the kids, you can also add some diced crystallized ginger. All these ingredients come together to create a delicious treat that's packed with vitamins and minerals. So go ahead, whip up a batch of fruitcake for your family this weekend and enjoy the sweet satisfaction of watching them devour it! Bon Appetit!

When it comes to assembling the cake, start by preheating your oven to 350°F (176°C) and greasing an 8-inch (20 cm) square baking pan. In a large bowl, combine 1½ cups diced dried pineapple, 1½ cups raisins, 1 cup diced dried apricots, heaping 1 cup chopped dates, and a heaping cup of candied red cherries. If desired for extra zing and fun for the kids, add $^1/^3$ cup crystallized ginger. Mix all these ingredients until they're evenly distributed throughout the batter.

Next, pour the mixture into the prepared baking pan and spread it evenly with a spatula or the back of a spoon. Bake for 40-45 minutes, or until the top is golden brown and a toothpick inserted into center comes out clean. Allow to cool in the pan for 10-15 minutes before removing from pan and transferring to a cooling rack.

Serve your fruitcake warm with a dollop of whipped cream or ice cream, if desired. It can also be enjoyed at room temperature and stored in an airtight container at room temperature for up to 4 days. Enjoy!

Happy baking!

Coconut Peanut Butter Balls

Coconut peanut butter balls are a sweet and healthy snack for kids that can be made with only a few simple ingredients. With an easy-to-follow recipe, these delicious treats are the perfect way to satisfy everyone's cravings without compromising nutrition or taste!

To make coconut peanut butter balls, start by combining 1 cup of quick oats, ¾ cup of unsweetened shredded coconut (plus more for rolling), ½ cup of smooth peanut butter (natural and unsalted), ½ cup peanuts (dry-roasted and unsalted), ¼ cup packed pitted Medjool dates, ¾ teaspoon cinnamon and ¾ teaspoon fine sea salt in a medium bowl. Stir until everything is well combined. Then add 3 tablespoons of coconut oil and mix again until everything is evenly distributed.

Once your ingredients are ready, start forming the balls by scooping up a spoonful of the mixture and rolling it firmly between your hands. Roll each ball in some extra shredded coconut for extra flavor and texture. Place them on a lined baking tray, cover with plastic wrap and refrigerate for 30 minutes to allow them to firm up. Your delicious coconut peanut butter balls are now ready to enjoy!

A great source of protein and fiber, these energizing bites make an excellent snack or treat that even picky eaters will love. Plus, they're easy to take along with you on-the-go for when hunger strikes! So there's no excuse not to whip up a batch of these tasty coconut peanut butter balls. Enjoy!

Raspberry Jelly

Nothing beats homemade raspberry jelly! It's the perfect healthy dessert recipe for kids of all ages. With only a few ingredients and easy-to-follow steps, you can make your own raspberry jelly in no time.

To get started, you'll need 3 pounds of raspberries, 1 ½ cups of water, sugar (to taste), 2 tablespoons of fresh lemon juice and a pinch of coarse salt. Combine all these ingredients into a large pot over medium heat and bring it to a simmer. Cook for about 20 minutes or until thickened, stirring occasionally to prevent scorching. Once the mixture has cooled down slightly, strain it through a fine mesh strainer to remove any seeds and pulp.

Now that you have your delicious raspberry jelly, you can use it to top pancakes, waffles or ice cream. You could also make your own homemade jam tarts and jellied fruits with this recipe. Enjoy!

Happy cooking! :)

Vanilla Pudding

Making a delicious vanilla pudding doesn't have to be time-consuming or complicated. With just a few simple ingredients, you can easily whip up a healthy dessert that both adults and kids will love.

To make the best vanilla pudding ever, you'll need the following ingredients: whole milk, cornstarch, salt, sugar, egg yolks, butter and pure vanilla extract.

Start by whisking together your dry ingredients in a medium-sized saucepan over medium heat-this includes the cornstarch, sugar and salt. Then add the egg yolks and stir until everything is combined. Gradually pour in your milk and cook on low to medium heat while stirring constantly until it thickens. Add the butter and stir until it melts. Finally, add the pure vanilla extract for an extra kick of flavor.

The end result is a sweet and creamy pudding that will make your taste buds happy! You can enjoy this delicious treat as-is or top with some fresh fruit or whipped cream for added flavor. Enjoy! This easy-to-make vanilla pudding is sure to become a family favorite in no time! So why not give it a try tonight? You won't regret it!

Chocolate Peanut Butter Bars

Ingredients

1/2 cup (115g) salted butter, melted*
1 cup (120g) graham cracker crumbs (about 8 full sheet graham crackers)*
2 cups (240g) confectioners' sugar.
1 cup + 2 Tablespoons (280g) creamy peanut butter, divided.
1 cup (180g) semi-sweet chocolate chips.

These Chocolate Peanut Butter Bars are the perfect healthy treat for kids. With just a few simple ingredients, you can have a delicious dessert that's ready in no time! Start by melting the butter and adding it to graham cracker crumbs and confectioners' sugar in a bowl. Mix together until combined. Reserve 2 Tablespoons of peanut butter for later and then add the rest to the bowl with the other ingredients. Stir everything together until fully incorporated. Line an 8x8 inch baking pan with parchment paper and spread the mixture evenly into it. In a small microwavable bowl, melt chocolate chips in 15-second intervals, stirring in between each interval until melted and smooth. Spread the melted chocolate over the top of the peanut butter bars and then drizzle the reserved peanut butter over the top. Allow to cool for at least an hour before cutting into bars and serving. Enjoy!

Happy snacking!

I want to take a moment to express my heartfelt gratitude for your recent purchase of my recipe book. As a passionate food lover, nothing makes me happier than sharing my favorite recipes with others. Your decision to invest in my book not only supports my dream, but also shows your commitment to expanding your culinary horizons.

I sincerely hope that the recipes in the book will inspire you to try new things and add some excitement to your meals.

Thank you again for your support and for being a part of this journey with me. I hope my book will bring you many happy and delicious moments in the kitchen.

www.ingramcontent.com/pod-product-compliance
Lightning Source LLC
Chambersburg PA
CBHW041150110526
44590CB00027B/4186